AMAZING Deserts AROUND THE WORLD

by Rachel Castro

raintree
a Capstone company — publishers for children

Raintree is an imprint of Capstone Global Library Limited, a company incorporated in England and Wales having its registered office at 264 Banbury Road, Oxford, OX2 7DY – Registered company number: 6695582

www.raintree.co.uk
myorders@raintree.co.uk

Text © Capstone Global Library Limited 2020
The moral rights of the proprietor have been asserted.

All rights reserved. No part of this publication may be reproduced in any form or by any means (including photocopying or storing it in any medium by electronic means and whether or not transiently or incidentally to some other use of this publication) without the written permission of the copyright owner, except in accordance with the provisions of the Copyright, Designs and Patents Act 1988 or under the terms of a licence issued by the Copyright Licensing Agency, Barnard's Inn, 86 Fetter Lane, London, EC4A 1EN (www.cla.co.uk). Applications for the copyright owner's written permission should be addressed to the publisher.

Edited by Claire Vanden Branden
Designed by Becky Daum
Original illustrations © Capstone Global Library Limited 2020
Production by Dan Peluso
Originated by Capstone Global Library Ltd

ISBN 978 1 4747 7466 6 (hardback)
ISBN 978 1 4747 8119 0 (paperback)

British Library Cataloguing in Publication Data
A full catalogue record for this book is available from the British Library.

Acknowledgements
We would like to thank the following for permission to reproduce photographs: Alamy: National Geographic Creative, 16–17; iStockphoto: agustavop, 26–27, AlexmarPhoto, 5, 30–31, AvatarKnowmad, 15, Pavliha, 9, Ron_Thomas, 6–7, 28, SteveByland, 12–13, tonda, 10–11; Shutterstock Images: 2630ben, 23, Armin Rose, 18–19, Anton Foltin, cover, Jose Luis Stephens, 24–25, Vaclav Sebek, 20–21.

Every effort has been made to contact copyright holders of material reproduced in this book. Any omissions will be rectified in subsequent printings if notice is given to the publisher.

All the internet addresses (URLs) given in this book were valid at the time of going to press. However, due to the dynamic nature of the internet, some addresses may have changed, or sites may have changed or ceased to exist since publication. While the author and publisher regret any inconvenience this may cause readers, no responsibility for any such changes can be accepted by either the author or the publisher.

Printed and bound in the United Kingdom.

CONTENTS

CHAPTER ONE
AMAZING DESERTS.......... 4

CHAPTER TWO
HOT DESERTS................. 8

CHAPTER THREE
COLD DESERTS 14

CHAPTER FOUR
COASTAL DESERTS 22

Glossary 28
Top deserts to visit 29
Activity 30
Find out more 32
Index 32

CHAPTER 1

AMAZING Deserts

One-third of Earth's land is desert. Deserts can be hot or cold. But they are always dry.

Deserts get fewer than 25 centimetres (10 inches) of rain a year.

Deserts can be sandy.

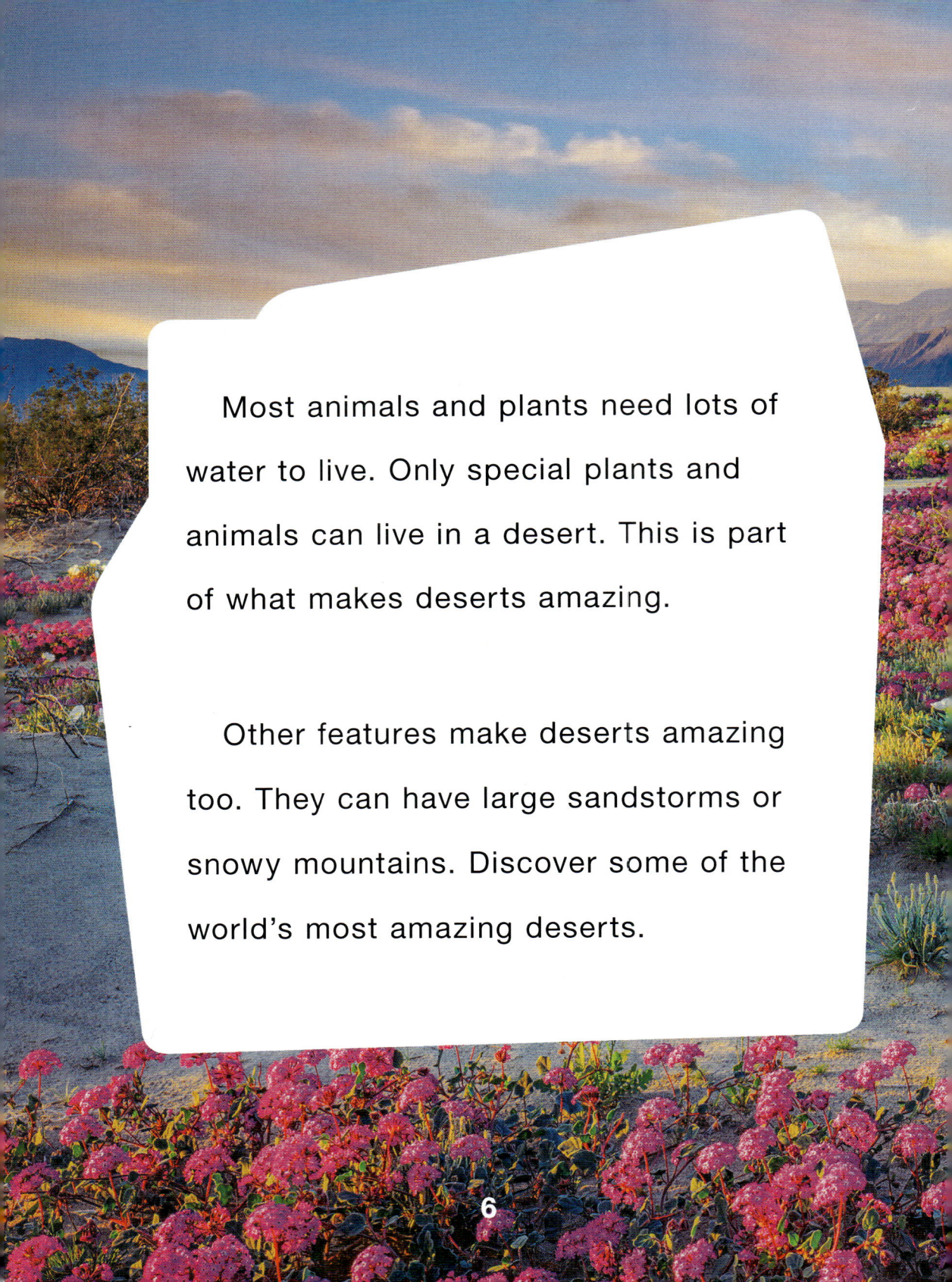

Most animals and plants need lots of water to live. Only special plants and animals can live in a desert. This is part of what makes deserts amazing.

Other features make deserts amazing too. They can have large sandstorms or snowy mountains. Discover some of the world's most amazing deserts.

Some of the most beautiful plants grow in deserts.

7

CHAPTER 2

HOT Deserts

The Sahara Desert is the largest hot desert on Earth. It covers much of North Africa.

The wind is very strong in the Sahara. It makes storms that can last for days. These storms bring large clouds of **dust** and sand. Some of these clouds are more than 1,600 kilometres (1,000 miles) long.

Some sandstorms in the Sahara travel at 40 kilometres (25 miles) per hour.

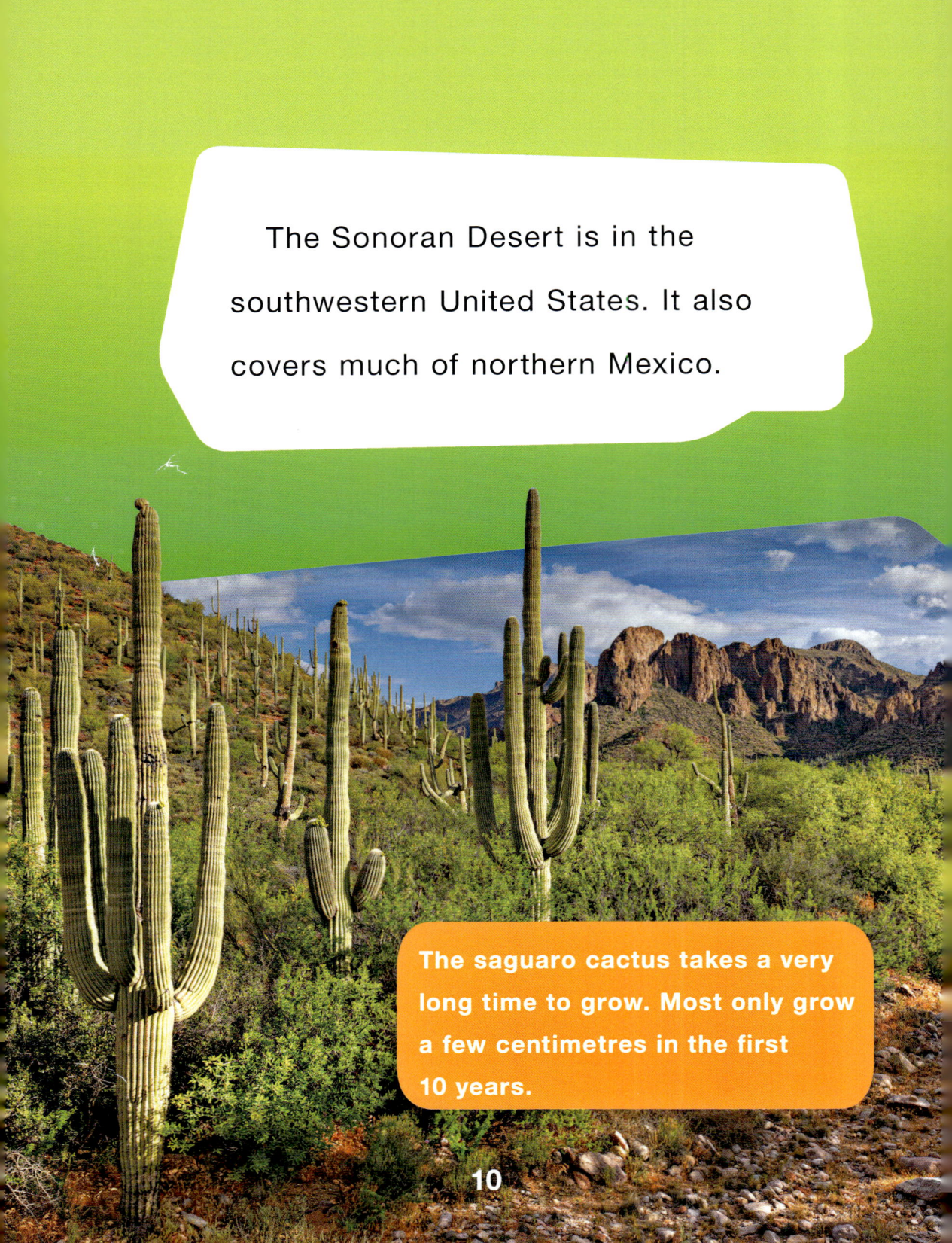

The Sonoran Desert is in the southwestern United States. It also covers much of northern Mexico.

The saguaro cactus takes a very long time to grow. Most only grow a few centimetres in the first 10 years.

OLD CACTI

The saguaro can live for 200 years. Most don't grow arms until they are 95 years old.

There are many plants in the Sonoran. The saguaro **cactus** can only grow here. These cacti can reach 15 metres (50 feet) tall. They are the largest cacti in the United States. Some have more than 50 arms!

A Gila monster lives mainly underground. It leaves its burrow to find food and to warm itself in the desert sun.

Many interesting animals live in the Sonoran Desert. It is the only place in the United States where jaguars live. The Gila monster is a large lizard found in the Sonoran Desert. It can be up to 60 centimetres (2 feet) long.

CHAPTER 3

COLD Deserts

Not all deserts are hot. Some deserts are cold. They have ice and snow. Cold deserts can be found near mountains.

The Great Basin Desert is the largest desert in the United States. It is also the only cold desert in the country.

Some trees in the Great Basin Desert are more than 5,000 years old.

The Gobi Desert covers parts of Mongolia and China. It is the largest desert in Asia. It is dry because of the Himalayas. These mountains block rain clouds, which means rain can't reach the desert.

Most of this desert is not sandy. It is rocky. Scientists often dig there. They have found fossils of dinosaur eggs!

An unusual bear lives in the Gobi Desert. It is called the Gobi bear. There are only a few of these bears left in the world.

The Gobi bear was first discovered in 1943.

There are only two polar deserts on Earth. They are the Antarctic and the Arctic.

The Antarctic is the largest desert in the world. It is at the South Pole. There is little sunlight here and it is very cold. Almost all of the desert is made up of an **ice sheet**.

The Arctic Desert is at the North Pole. It is made up of many islands. It gets the same amount of rain and snow as the Sahara.

POLAR BEARS

Polar bears can be found only in the Arctic.

Polar bears have thick fur that keeps them warm in the extreme cold of the Arctic.

CHAPTER 4
COASTAL Deserts

Coastal deserts are by the ocean. Very little rain falls in coastal deserts, but the cool sea air forms **fog**.

Animals and plants have special ways to get water from the fog. Some animals drink droplets of water from the fog that settles on their bodies.

The Namib Desert is a coastal desert in Africa. It is the world's oldest desert. It is millions of years old.

Elephants that live here have bigger feet and longer legs than other elephants. This helps them to walk through sand.

Elephants almost always travel in a herd.

The Atacama Desert is in Chile. Parts of it have not had rain for more than 400 years. It is the world's driest desert.

The Atacama is next to the Amazon. The Amazon is a rainforest. The driest place on Earth is next to one of the wettest!

Wild donkeys live in part of the Atacama Desert.

Many rocks in the Atacama Desert are red, similar to Mars.

Scientists say that the Atacama Desert is like Mars. They study it to try to learn if there is a chance of life on Mars.

STARRY NIGHTS

The Atacama is a great place for stargazing. The skies are very clear there.

GLOSSARY

cactus
plant with a thick stem that has fleshy tissues that hold in water

dust
fine particles in the air

fog
cloud at ground level that has water droplets in the air

ice sheet
permanent layer of ice that covers a large area of land

TOP DESERTS TO VISIT

ANTARCTIC DESERT
Bundle up before taking a trip to the largest desert in the world.

ARCTIC DESERT
Come to the Arctic to see the only place where polar bears live.

ATACAMA DESERT
Look at the clear night sky in the world's driest desert.

GOBI DESERT
Join in on the hunt for dinosaur fossils.

NAMIB DESERT
Visit the world's oldest desert and see its interesting elephants.

SAHARA DESERT
Experience a sandstorm close up.

SONORAN DESERT
See the largest cacti in the United States in this hot desert.

ACTIVITY

MAKE A SAND DUNE!

Sand dunes are found in deserts. They are formed by strong winds. This activity shows how sand dunes are formed among rocks, trees or shrubs in a desert.

WHAT YOU'LL NEED:
- sand
- shallow shoebox or roasting tray (at least 5 cm deep)
- rock
- drinking straw

INSTRUCTIONS:

1. Clear a work area by covering a table with cloth or newspapers.

2. Pour sand into the shoebox or roasting tray. Use enough so that the bottom of the box or tray is completely covered.

3. Place a rock in the sand.

4. Gently shake the container until the sand is flat.

5. Use a drinking straw to blow the sand in various directions.

It will begin to pile up against the rock. The sand in the container will begin to form shapes, like sand dunes. Imagine the size of the dunes in the desert!

FIND OUT MORE

Books

Exploring Deserts: A Benjamin Blog and His Inquisitive Dog Investigation (Exploring Habitats with Benjamin Blog and His Inquisitive Dog), Anita Ganeri (Raintree, 2015)

Desert Climates (Focus on Climate Zones), Cath Senker (Raintree, 2018)

Deserts (Explorer Travel Guides), Nick Hunter (Raintree, 2013)

Website

www.dkfindout.com/uk/earth/deserts

Find out more about deserts.

INDEX

Amazon 24
Antarctic Desert 19
Arctic Desert 19–20
Atacama Desert 24, 27

elephants 23

Gila monster 13
Gobi bear 17
Gobi Desert 16–17
Great Basin Desert 15

Mars 27

Namib Desert 22–23

rain 4, 16, 20, 22, 24

saguaro 11
Sahara Desert 8–9, 20
sandstorms 6, 9
Sonoran Desert 10–11, 13